scars & lyres

poetry by ww harris

QUILLKEEPERS PRESS

Copyright © ww harris, 2022
Book Cover Design by stephanie lamb
Edit by christopher howell
Format by Quillkeepers Press, LLC

ISBN: 979-8-9868389-1-5

Published by Quillkeepers Press, LLC
PO Box 10236
Casa Grande, AZ 85130

i would like to thank christopher howell, jonathan johnson, laura read, joshua phillips, chris green, mark turcotte, eric selinger, miles harvey, marilyn kallet, jessie janeshek, & arthur smith for their instruction and recommendations throughout the many years & programs it took to get me to finally write this

i would like to dedicate this book to everyone i have ever loved music with

in the street of the sky night walks scattering poems—
ee cummings

i mispronounce myself—kazim ali

we're flowers not just people—dean young

poets are not to blame for how things are—homer

table of contents

new scars

old lyres

new scars

heroin

my days boil on the end of a match

      my heartbeat echoes a slow reprise

          another song i won't remember

      another chorus of regret

fading in & out of time's radio

      my blood slamming in my ears

i have made a cairn of my bones

      libations i bubble in aluminum foil

          i cup storms of poison in my palms

moon a dime bag i'll never reach

time speaks her golden tongue

smoke & consonance

her lips

unfolding in the sky

where our days

are leaves of bright fire

our shadows

pressing for a pulse

singing

into ragged moonlight

each breath

a shimmering constellation

our hearts are cups

we can never fill

suicide

burst of flash engulfing the room in fire & silence
your head   a blond balloon   you make mortal

stabs of sad lightning & empty thunder wake you
with smoldering skulldust   & starmatter

& distilled wings of angels   with shining lyres
& scars   one afternoon   as you're trying

to make a bong   out of an apple
you press your lips into a smoking horizon

you erase your tongue   on this pyre of iron
& cordite   bright buckshot blooming

with metal sunlight   the last time
i see you   we smoke a joint in my parents' backyard

your eyes blue chandeliers   i can still feel
the fire between my fingers   as we make smoke rings

gray & fat & filled with   blood & don't

box of rain

tongue a bomb

that won't stop

blooming

box of webbed tissue

& veins

& imperfect song

worthless assonance

& consonance

pink box behind my lips

pink wing beating

featherless bones

each word

its own inky box

of rusty teeth

& onomatopoeia

my lisp

a refrain of insecurity

of loneliness

& lightning

a sparkplug misfiring

against bone box

of my skull

against chambered box

of my heart

& its ignorance

of sunshine

of my ribs'

whitespace

my lisp

a lot like running

naked

through uncertain

rain before an eclipse

catching all but sunlight

wrapped in a gauze

of syllables

each word

a minefield

come as you are

cupping woodgrain & iron i chase

unheard horses into smoke & lightning

gun

rainbow bridge peeling from my skin

gun

lips an open vowel

gun

grief swallowed in

gunfire

grief a sheet i wrap myself in each night

as i count buckshot & stardust

gun

hands outstretched as if offering

cordite fire to a god

gun

blonde hair & brain matter

gun

smell of oil & wooden stock

gun

trigger a tooth i can't stop pulling

gun

tasting cold metal

gun

even the palms of angels

can't wipe my scars clean

gun

blossoming of booming beauty

gun

my knees bending as if in penitence

gun

wet & sighing lips open

gun

as if in a final

no

tattoo'd lady

wing of ink / tapestry of time / splintering minutes
                    with hammers / with teeth & ripping kisses /
                                    with winding sheets

& cheap hotel keys / eyelids falling like machetes / silence
                    severing promises / burnt by inevitability /
                                    trading caresses & tears

for songs i used to sing / tongue a torch of fire
                    of pink cigarette butts & broken feathers /
                                    i choke

on empty wine bottles / on temporary smiles & on ink
                    on this choir of quiet screams /
                                    a harmony of impermanence & skin

& the thorns of spring / kneeling before panting breaths
                    gasping in quarter notes & eighths /
                                    piercing myself on

your reflection / on tilework & black tv's / our lonely throats
                    trilling tulips / our lungs red jars /
                                    we fill with dreaming

nightswimming

swaddling in the wordlessness
of day & night

out from bursting womb
comes swimming

purple skin
lip & lung blueblack oxygen

breath a gasp around his neck
noose of umbilical quiet

suffocated by time's fangs
she wakes me up crying

i don't remember what time it is
but recall shards of night

still being eaten by day
& the horrible quiet of her tears

water breaking

he deserves a name

i tell the nurses

there wasn't time

for his mother & me to marry

& through a veil of hot tears

i imagine my son

wandering in the night

lost & not knowing what name to call

swimming alone

through the ether

in the quiet of eternity's bell

from time-to-time

i imagine my son

an owl

swimming through the night

each gust of wind

each wing's flap

a breath

manic depression

my name labeled ink

stickered to a pill bottle

the word *manic*

a crescendo

of butterfly wings

hyphen-halved

before *depression*

like a lip torn in a kiss

synaptic lightning

falling into a void

erasure of sunshining blister

quilt of freezing sighs

a bowl of skulls

so many discarded

calendars & empty

cigarette packs

all of it

a wound

i can't stop licking

helpless

nooses of interstates

& seasons

decaying clouds

& concrete roads

breathing little more than wind

days are thorns

we can't stop pulling

misery an eye

we can't blind

hope a color

we can never see

rugged light

shining against wings

another yesterday dissolving

lyrics

i can't ever remember

eleanor rigby

it's been three months

since my son died

& people ask me

how how how

their questions

exploding like shoe bombs

i look around the floor

i passed out on

it's the bathroom of the house

my first wife & i shared

i never drank before my son died

now i never stop

i pour whiskey

red & lonely in my pink

sailor moon thermos

i see my face

in the bathroom mirror

& smash all the lightbulbs

in the house

eighteen

whitespace   razored onto tiny
mirror water   crossing roads

    of bones   to powdered interstices
    of nod & numb

life tossed aside for rolled
dollar bills & nights eating

    days   eating my heart's horizons
    with each breath i choke on

what i have become   but
can't stop being   what i am

dollar bill

stars anesthetized

from whitespaced powder

from shining lyres or scars

in an open field

dandelions burning

with their own gold

lined white green bill

or red slamming slamming

in my chest

green memoir

of regret & ash

wading into flames

like a kiss

that won't stop bleeding

or an old heartbeat

waiting to be held

an atomic blast

in montage

eight-ball a sea

of three & a half

white grams

of night twisting

into a carousel of numb

of chopped lines

i rub with a cigarette filter

like i'm erasing

ideograms i can't remember

i fold twenty dollar

bills into squares

& hide them

from myself

each twenty

a gram of star milk

each square

a plastic-wrapped swan

i'd tear apart

with key-bumps

& razorblades

coating the inside

of a dollar

the inside of my nose

& throat

& my life squandered

like tears flung

against a wall of clouds

holding dollar to mirror

to a copy of *junkie*

to anything

to hold this weight

this angry halo

bloody as my nose

creep

i'm half the man i used to be
i thought as the jailor weighed me
the heroin had folded me
into an origami of shadows
we'd go to jobsites
in my maroon station wagon
sold stolen sawblades
& framing hammers
to construction workers
then drove
across memphis' concrete face
for bitter brown stardust
in blue stamped paper
for a needle a spoon
burnt blueblack
by time's charring whisper

electrolite

skin between us pressing air
heartbeats & winding sheets

are skies filled with too few sparrows
& whitespaced clouds

countless blue morpho wings
tumbling from your lips

red & pink rushing blood
to your cheeks

smoking horses dance
in gray lamplight

the static hum of your touch
against time's bluing sparks

the wounded stars & ashes
we rub into our wings

the ghosts of our silhouettes
their mouths open as if in a wish

head with wings

i.   *scars*

i've been trying to die

for so long i forgot

how to live

i've been falling so long

my face streaked with clouds

my wings with blisters

of bitter powder

needle's sharp kiss

& shirt sleeve red

again

another scarlet stripe

before my wings collapse

my life heading

toward molten wax

into these waters

i boil myself

ii.   lyres

for years i begged

for something nobody

can give

wounded myself

on twenty-dollar tenths

i'd buy at the gates to graceland

on elvis presley boulevard

before heading back

to a shooting gallery

off raines avenue

my wings already

beginning to sizzle & smoke

with fire

i clasp in my palm

(i can't get no) satisfaction

smell of white & chemical

cigarette filter rubs against

altar of a cold mirror

cotton *squeak* against glass

at a gas station i leave my hood up

in a bad attempt at avoiding suspicion

waiting for plastic-wrapped death for

no sleep no sleep no sleep no sleep

my heart filled with whitespace

old lyres

rusty cage

i am driving

chicago to memphis

never gonna see

her again

never hear her

crying into a mirror

or breaking all the glasses

in the kitchen

never gonna cut

my fingers again

on the shards

of our marriage

& i know

my only chance at surviving

is to run

i'm just sobering up

in another jailhouse

& my skin

feels like it's burning

one minute then calving

off in frozen sheets

the next

i find my stash

a tiny wad

of brown scag

wrapped in a band-aid

between my toes

bitter phoenix i snort

& my heart stops

hurting for a few hours

& i run run run

in numbed stillness

i'm in my shitty apartment

in knoxville

i'm eating ice cream

& wild turkey

& tacking pictures

of paintings

to my walls

surrounding myself

with brushstrokes

filling in the whitespace

in my heart with walled

stanzas of pollock

& van gogh & dali

& these are the days

i learn i don't need

my feet to run

this bus i'm on can't go

slow enough

i'm riding west

through wrigleyville

i'm on my way

to see friends who tell

me i'll get past

this heartbreak in punk hair

& the part my heart

hates most is knowing

they're right

& i think again

how life is a series of keys

& sadness

& our lives are our favorite

tv show's worst rerun

looks like rain

you must have looked like an angel
but without some bullshit wing or lyre

i'll forever imagine how still still still
your lips were in the air

your rope & twist
your sky that looks like rain

i was told years later how you'd written
on the back of a photograph of us

folded in your pocket your suicide note
the shadow of your jeans swallowing

its letters as you float
not flying not falling

wing of noose & beam lifting you
impermanent as night or any other name

it's the worst day since yesterday

we break the lightbulb

bottom off

& rinse out

stardust-colored glass

& white paint debris

then smoke storms

of heroin

held in our palms

i've been in jail

three days

sweating junk out

as sadness explodes

all around inside of me

& somehow

i get sober

for three months

i'm at the hospital

my son's cold

& motionless

& in his visage

reflects my face

in breathless blue

blister in the sun

i was teaching
english 101
a few days ago
& a student sitting
in the front row
asked me
if i believe
in god
it is saint patty's day
it's 2009
i think
i'm dying
my hair green
clueless a & j are boiling
electric kool-aid
i drive over to j's house
& while i put some beer
in the fridge i see
the blue pitcher
by the milk & a couple
of capri sun packets
mushroom caps spinning
like tiny tawny sundials

in sugar & blueberry
we poured bright shots
while playing
air guitar to rush
& trying to force
more of the caps
down our throats
or nestling them
atop a shot glass
i don't remember
going outside
but found myself
in the backyard
on my knees in green grass
praying to the sun
balancing space & time
reality & unreality
on my fingertips
realizing this mathematical
singularity of the soul
this blister of our
being & its countless
carbon-based combinations

of molecules & rain

is just an illusion

of isolation

just tinny blood

& broken sunshine

& we're all

just tap dancing

under the proscenium

of mortality

while the stage

is being set

for someone else's fifth act

that's when i begin to vomit

in a near perfect circle

in the months to come

a halo of clovers

springs up

from the circle of grass

a faery ring

j's kids rub their fingers

in the emerald circle

all summer

picking 4-leaf clovers

while we drink cheap beer
& listen to more rush
anesthetizing the blister
behind our ribs
we call hearts
& for another year or so
i still worship the sun
i help his father & brothers
lower j into green earth
i hug his wife & 4 kids
i hold his mother's
thin hand
while the sun rotates
on its apathetic axis
uncaring j was sober 3 years
or that the heroin was cut
with fentanyl
so how do i tell
this kid in freshman comp
i lost any faith i ever had
like i lost my teeth
during childhood
one by one
& then all at once

suicide

i.   *scars*

spiraling sorrow

spinning lead

silver key

in flaming crimson

burning ball

of hollow no one

tearing itself

out of your skull

star that took years

to ignite

bursting torch

of yellow nothing

barrel-born

white infinity

leaving bloody silence

& smoke

in air choked

by your bright sadness

ii.   *lyres*

skull a halo of gunfire

& sky

blood & cordite

a hammer falling

upon an ocean

between your lips

the violence of sadness

last breath

an echoing barrel

of wet ellipses

palm gripping years

of misery like teeth

the warnings signed

in pints of red red red

the sharp edge

of deafening quiet

miss misery

no more dresses of tears

or skirts

of sleep sleep sleep

your souvenir scars

& your broken strings

a melody

of wellbutrin & lithium

your smile rows

of dopamine teeth

ripped from the bright

moons of your

serotonin skies

the needle & the damage done

epoch of gravestone & lost breath
blood blooming in plastic barrel

staining shirt sleeves & opus red
my years so many silent outros

epitaph of plunger & spike
existence ideograms held

by hyphen & etched into rock
this nothingness i hurry past

the shadows of hazy decades
of bloody lyres & shining scars

of running from yesterday
as i step into tomorrow's ghost

pictures of you

your wing a rainbow of ash

we rub into beaten mirrors

white shadow chanting

raw as morning

your silhouette

won't stop palms of ether

or the memories of poems

no tongue has sung

wake up

i held your belt tight so you'd

find a vein

traced your heartbeat's

shadow

sleep's sting a numb

release

from gnarled tears & bitter

teeth

in this green void of grass

we leave you

lowering you down with cords

the last time

i help tie you off

them bones

it was years before

i could write

about my mom's death

i told her once

how i knit sighs

with each breath

they feel

like silvery cobwebs

blistering with time

or air so high

it suffocates itself

we are born & die alone

but we get to burn

with such a blaze

we think we're gonna

glow forever

death is omnipresent

our end looms

over our shoulders

like clouds

that can't make up

their minds

which mountain

they should crash

into or if a bird

is a poem

with feathers

or if there's really a big

difference between a sonnet

& the rust

on my father's

old ford f-150

my mother in the seat

aside him

as cancers

pile atop each other

at the base of her skull

a cluster of angels

each of them

metastasized fists of carbon

& time & crows

& fate & bones

sun in an empty room

scars & souvenirs
packed in tiny
cardboard stanzas

memories & wishes
we bubble wrapped
in apologies

sweeping dreams
& dust out
the kitchen door

words we once
held like birds
are landmines exploding

shrapnel from pets
& the monostich
of our marriage

our hands

    are bowls of bones

holding empty keys

karma chameleon

blue canvas of iris
brushstrokes bleeding
interstates of teeth
owl feathers
dipped in gouache
tattooing the clouds
of my bones
every fracture
we sing alone
you spread translucent
dragonfly wings
fan the cheeks of twilight
birds collide
with an emptiness of sky
with an ocean of sparks
the embers of your hair
the insect of your smile
riding your carousel
of clouds & smoke
into the mists of memory
life is one long song
every heartbeat
an ideogram

tears in heaven

our teeth

our tears

are smoking constellations

face still-blue from pink

umbilical noose

against the dark tombstone

of sky's night

gathering fistfulls of cold

our fingers laced

like the stitching over a wound

holding the cityscape

of your heartbeat

like air cradles bird wings & song

stretching eternity's kiss

across the whitespace of years

i smear bloody letters

across the faces of stars

across years of blank canvases

your epitaph

your only song

choking on its hyphen

we make lyres

of our scars

notes

title for "heroin" from a song by the velvet underground

title for "time speaks her golden tongue" from a screaming trees song

title for "suicide" from a thin lizzy song

title for "box of rain" from a grateful dead song

title for "come as you are" from a nirvana song

title for "tattoo'd lady" from a rory gallagher song

title for "nightswimming" from a rem song

title for "eleanor rigby" from a song by the beatles

title for "eighteen" from an alice cooper song

title for "dollar bill" from a screaming trees song

title & italicized line for "creep" from a stone temple pilots song

title for "electrolite" from a rem song

title for "head with wings" from a morphine song

title for "(i can't get no) satisfaction" from a song by the rolling stones

title for "rusty cage" from a soundgarden song

title for "looks like rain" from a grateful dead song

title for "it's the worst day since yesterday" from a flogging molly song

title for "blister in the sun" from a velvet underground song

title for "suicide" from a thin lizzy song

title for "miss misery" from an elliott smith song

title for "the needle & the damage done" from a neil young song

title for "pictures of you" from a song by the cure

title for "wake up" from a mad season song

title for "them bones" from an alice in chains song

title for "sun in an empty room" from a song by the weakerthans

title for "karma chameleon" from a culture club song

title for "tears in heaven" from an eric clapton song

ww harris studied at University of Tennessee-Knoxville, DePaul University, and recently finished the MFA program at Eastern Washington University. His poems most recently appeared in North Dakota Quarterly and Bryant Literary Review and in 2021 won an International Merit Award from Atlanta Review.